AF411873

FRONT POCKETS

JONATHAN BONNER

The object pairs in this series are made to be carried in the front pockets of your trousers.

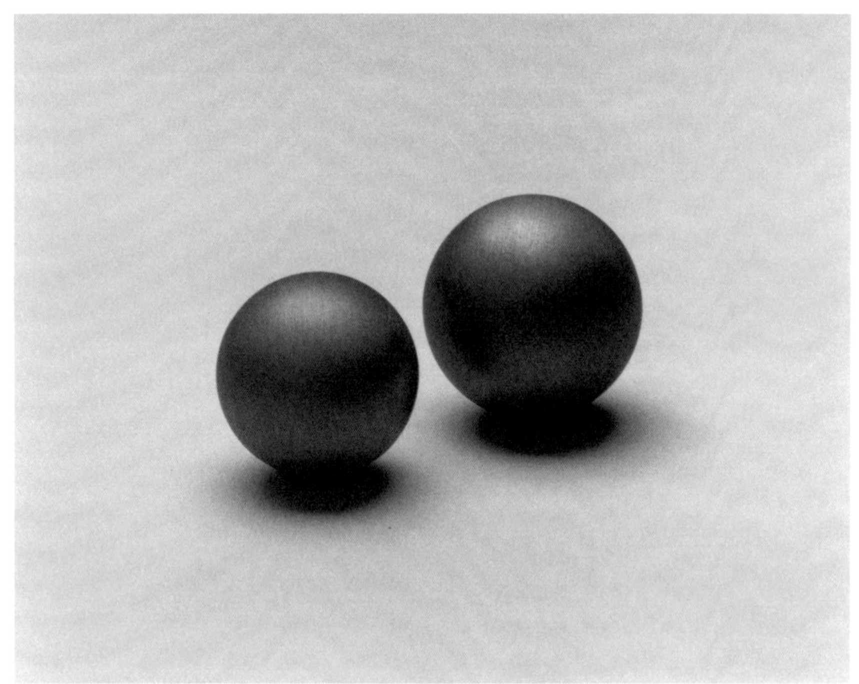

Graphite Pocket Balls

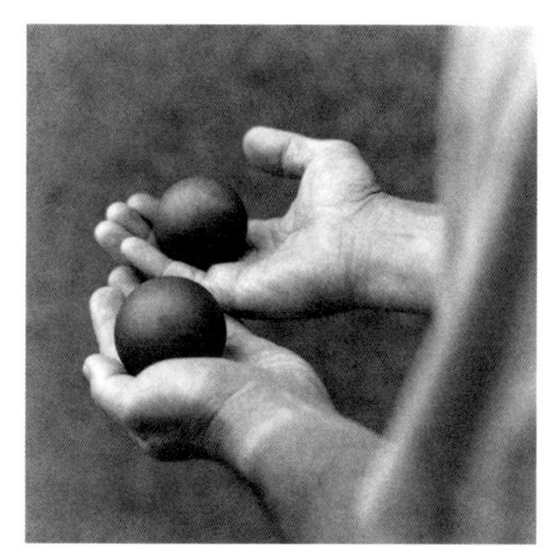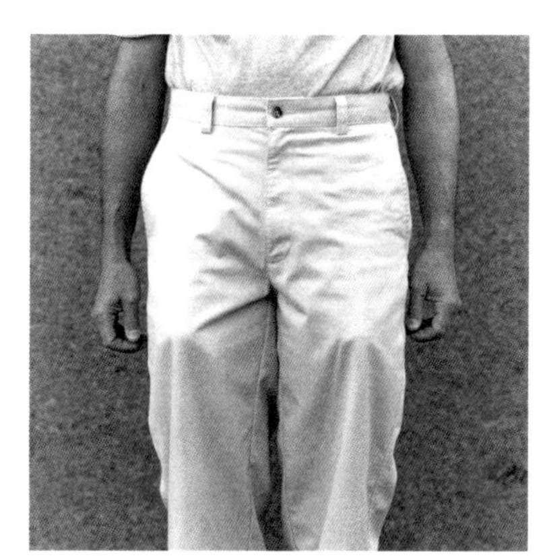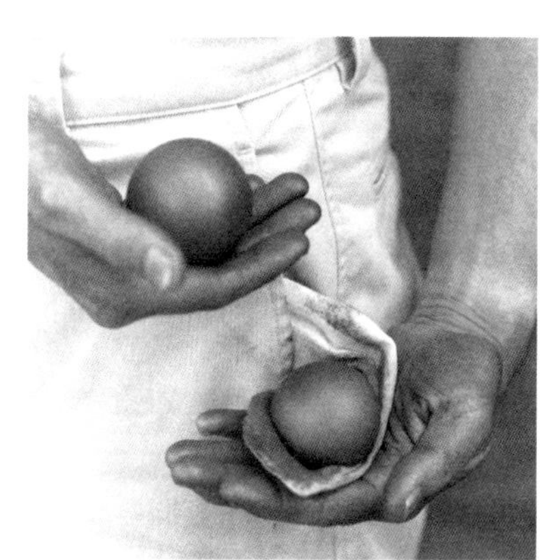

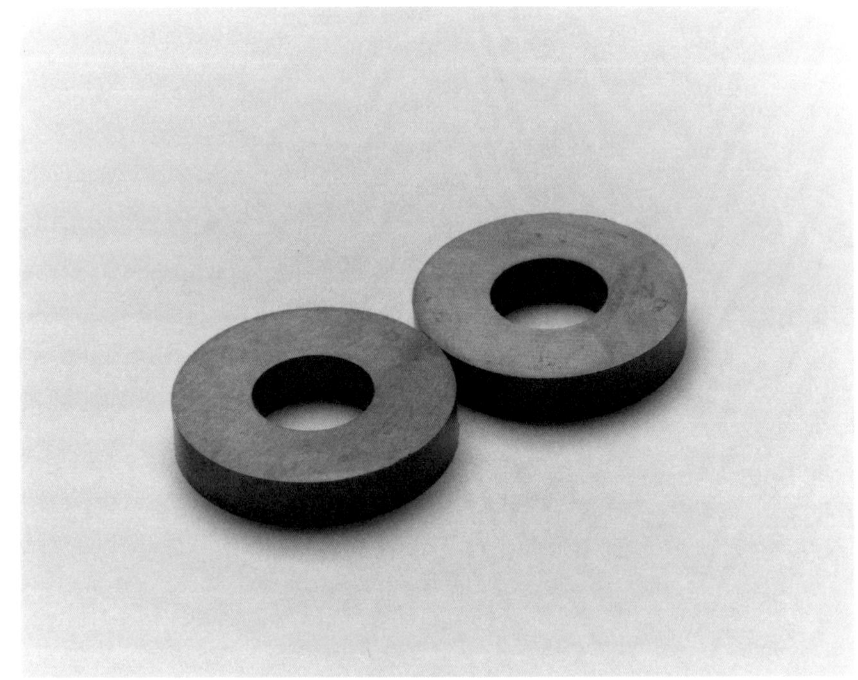

Pocket Magnets

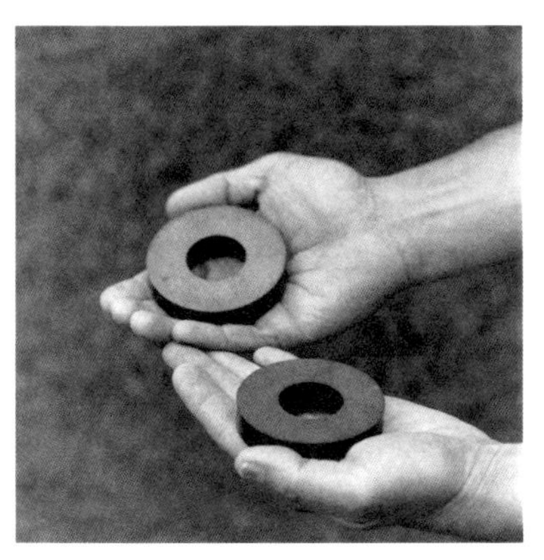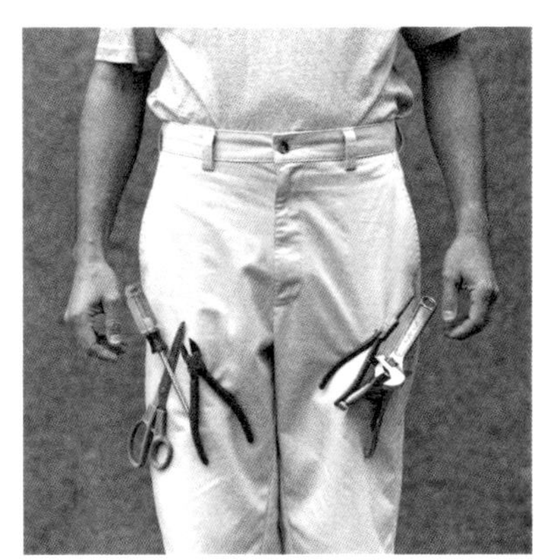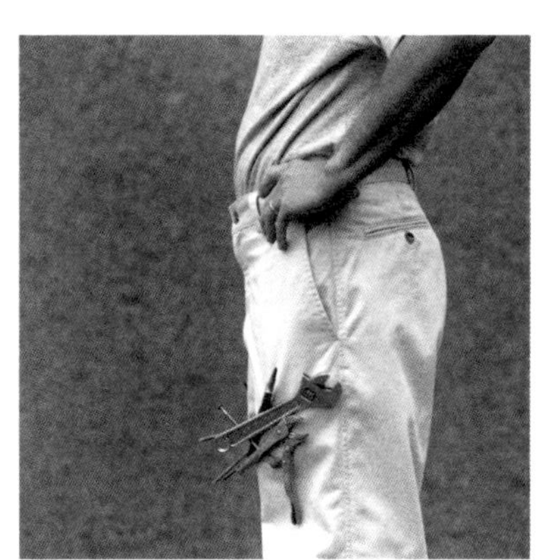

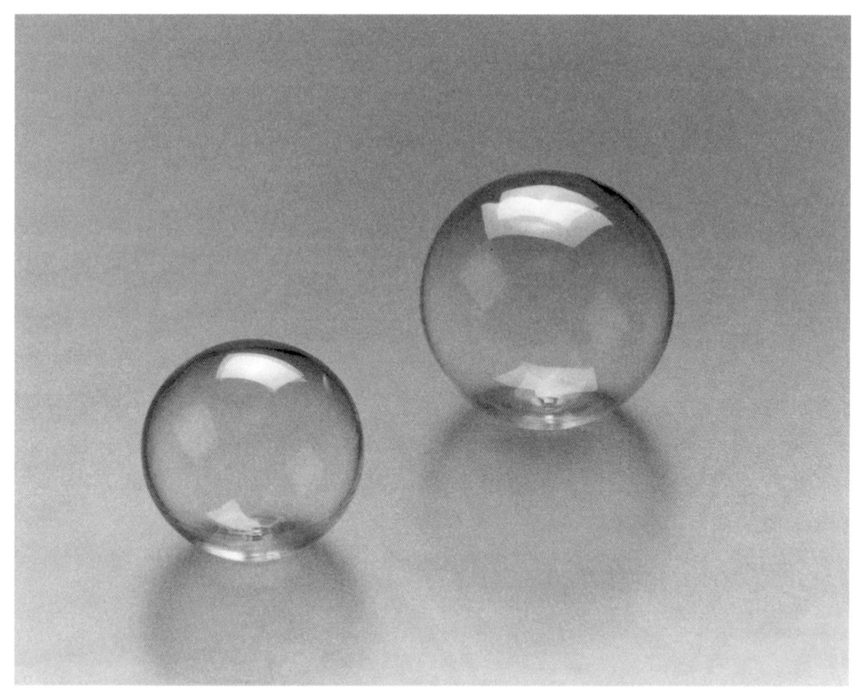

Glass Pocket Balls

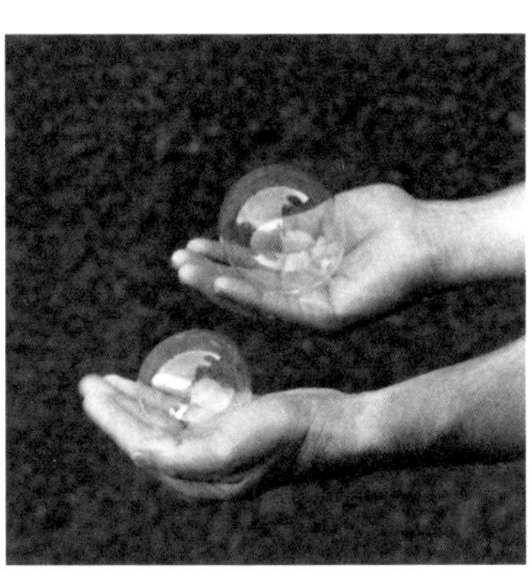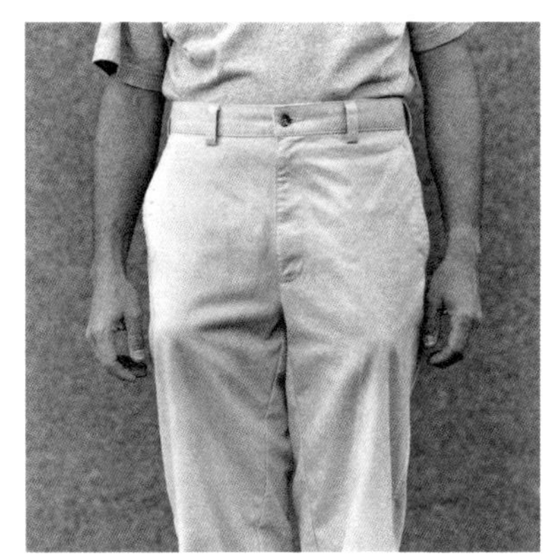

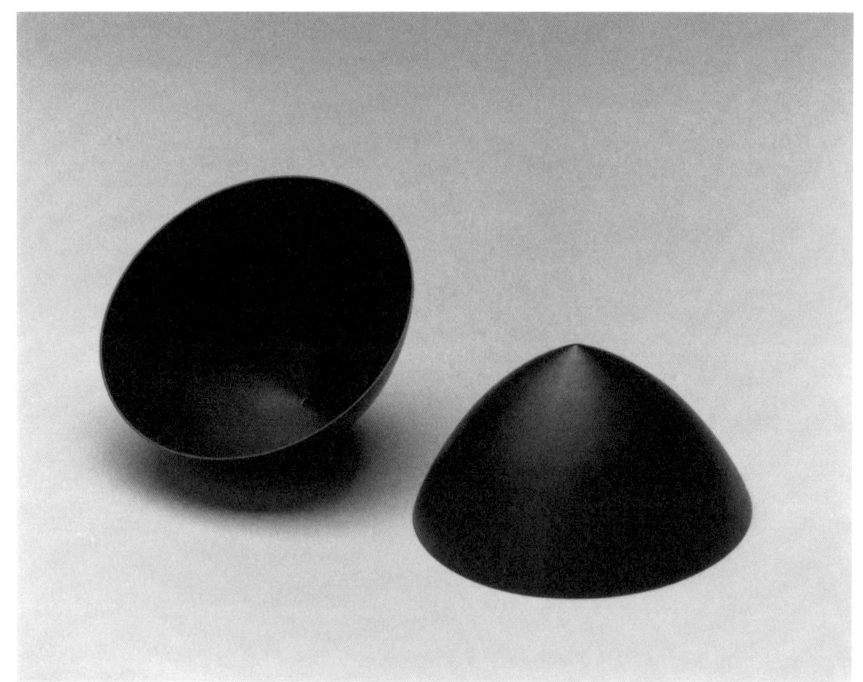

Ice Pocket Mounds

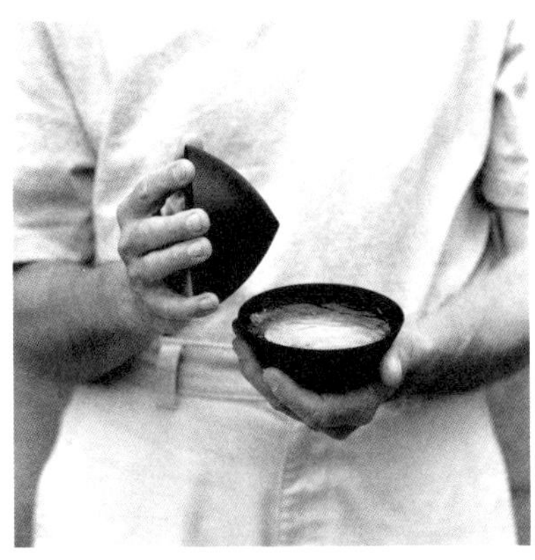
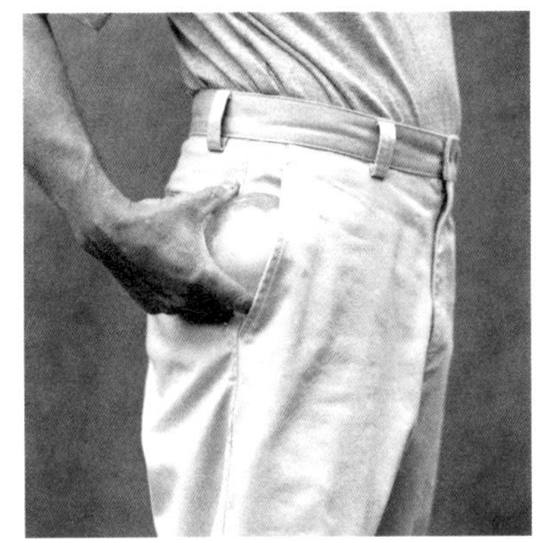
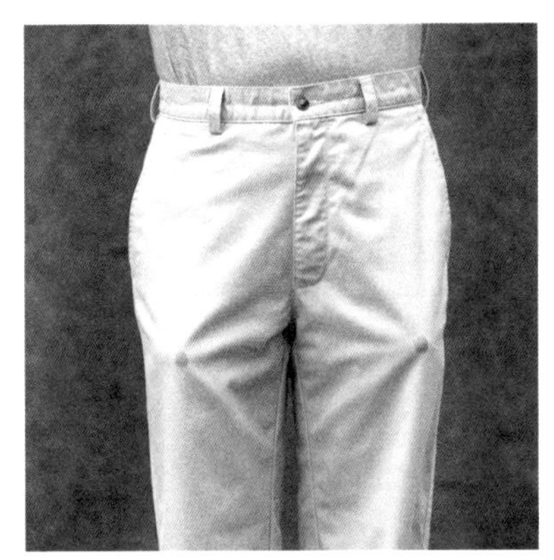
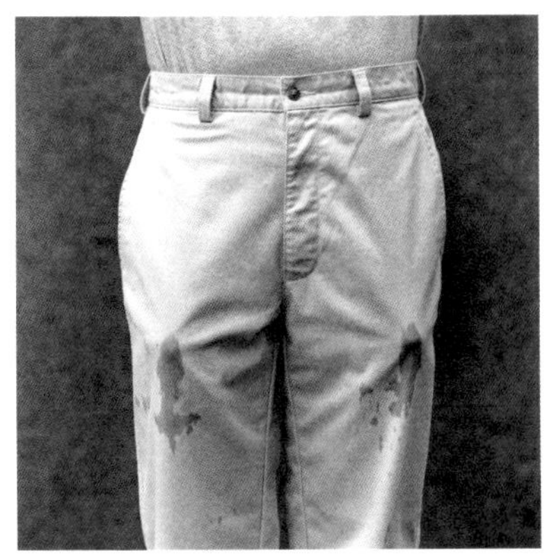
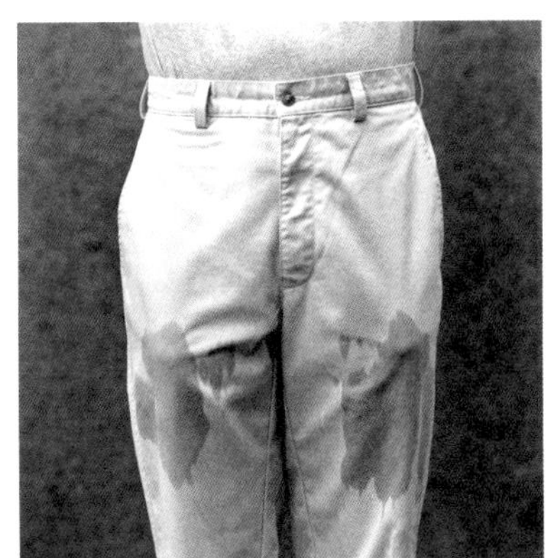
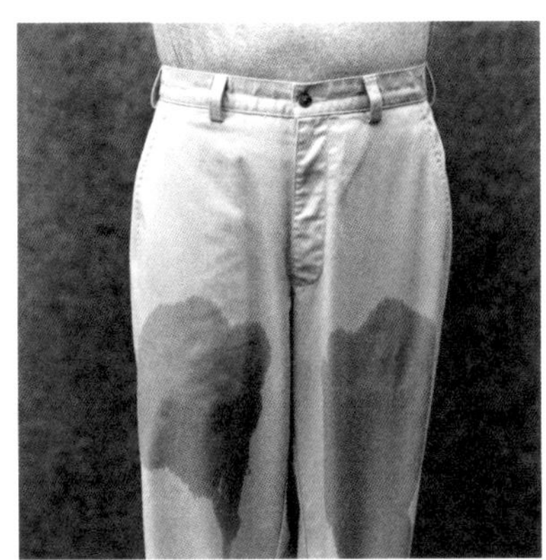

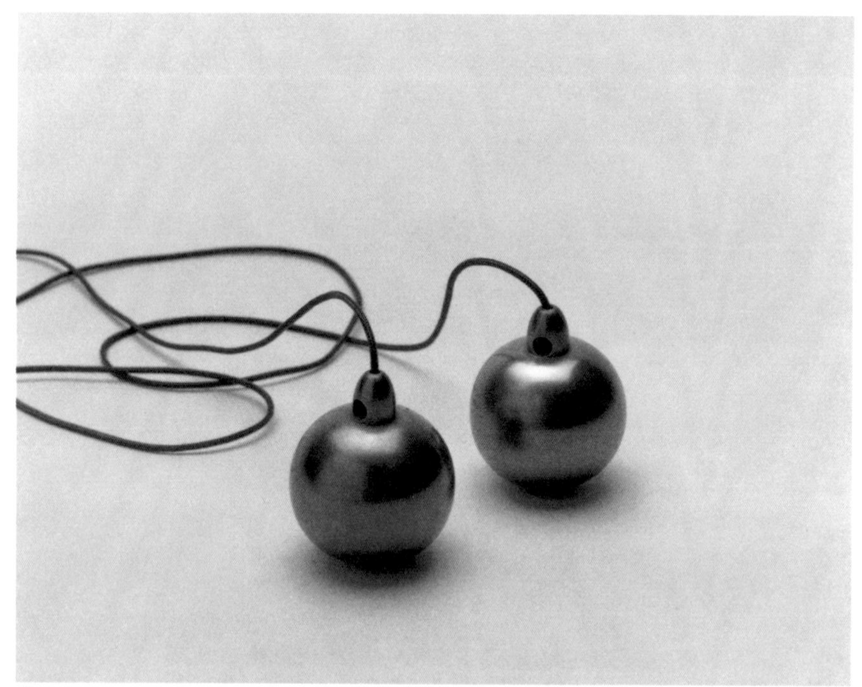

Pocket Counterweights

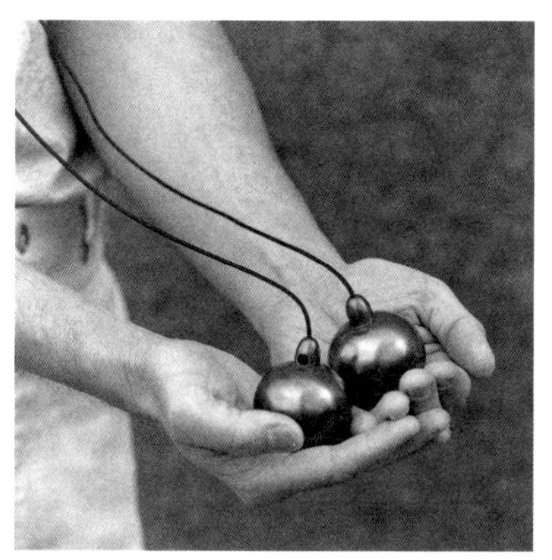
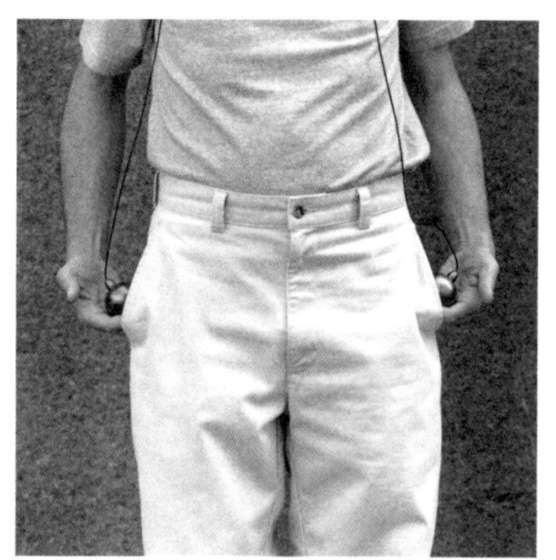
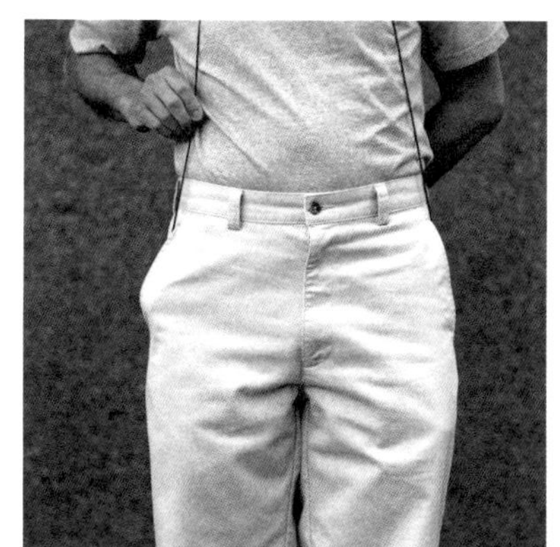
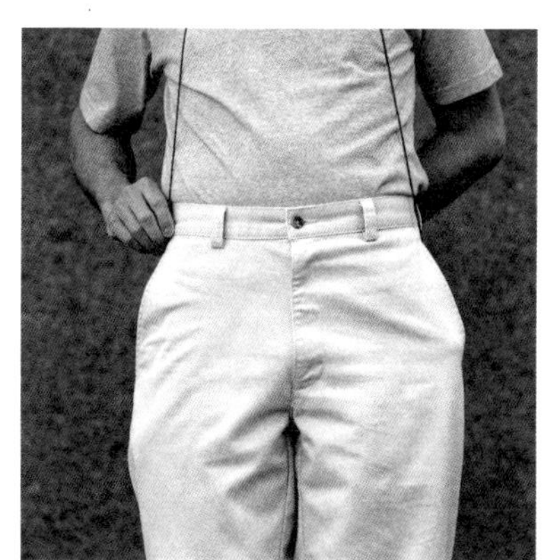
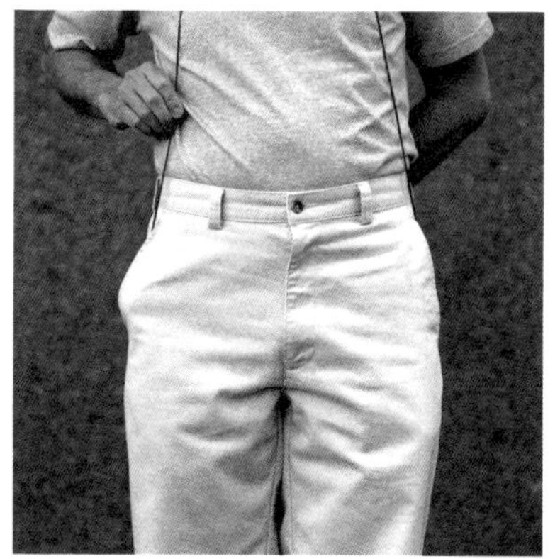

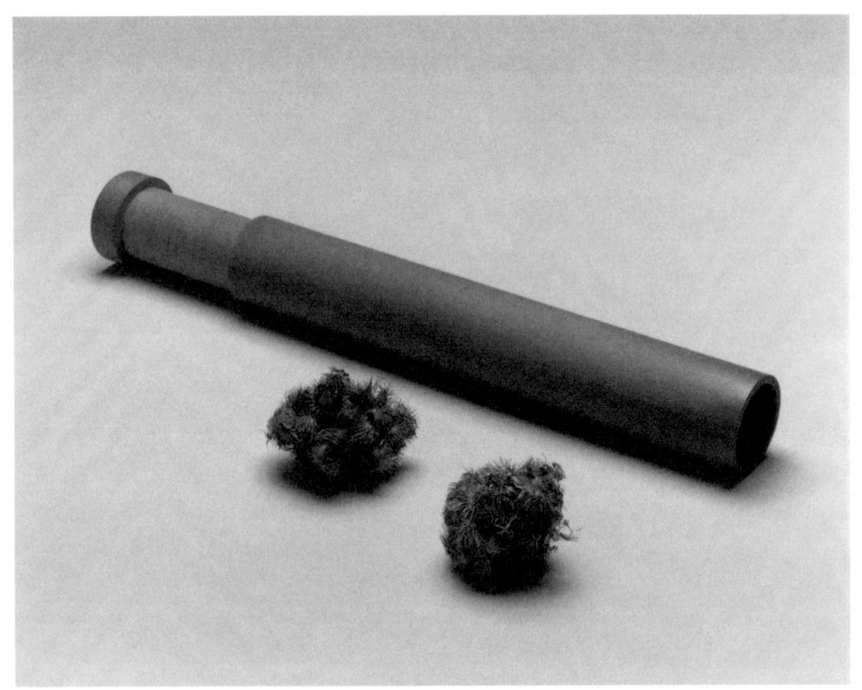

Pocket Burr Balls with Insertion Tube

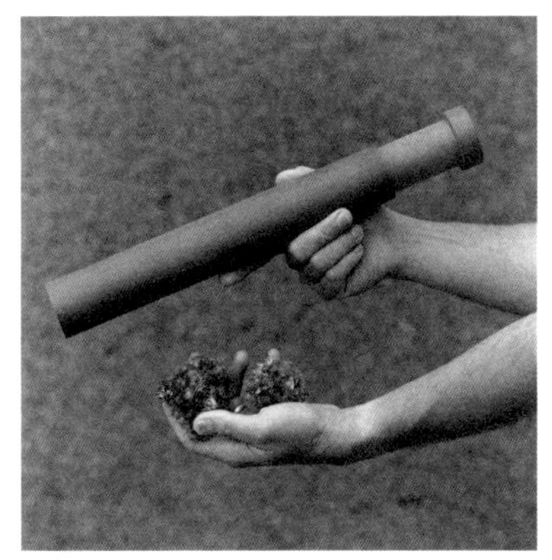

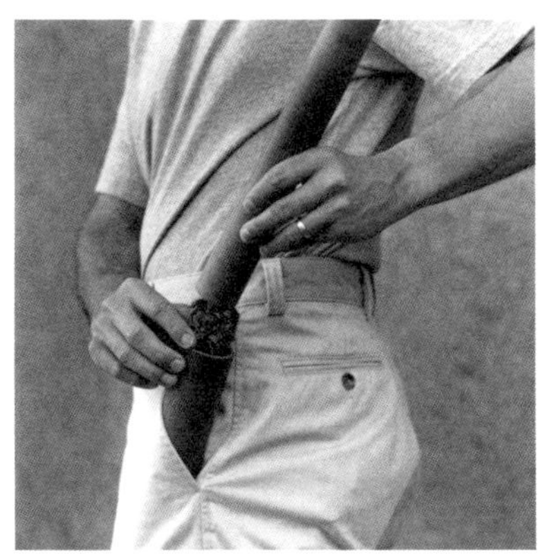
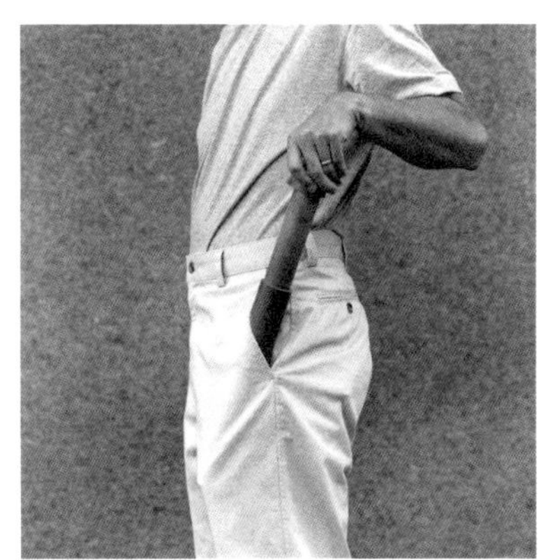
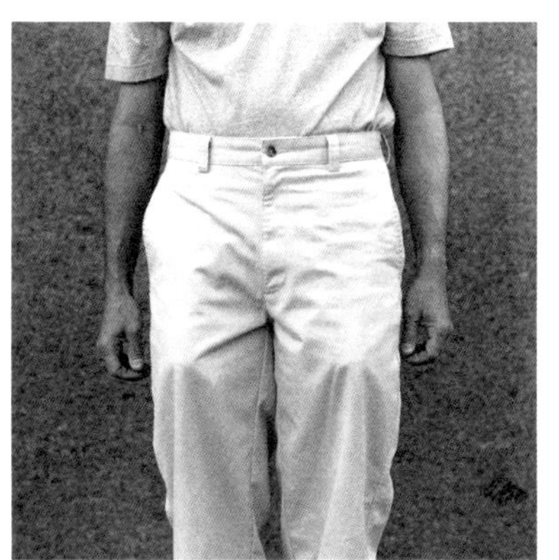

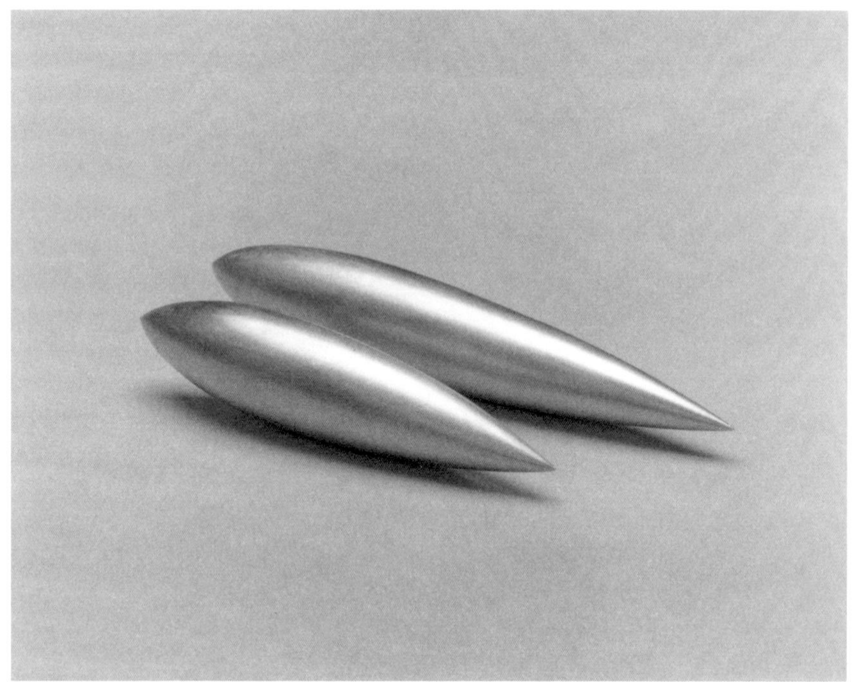

Pocket Weasels

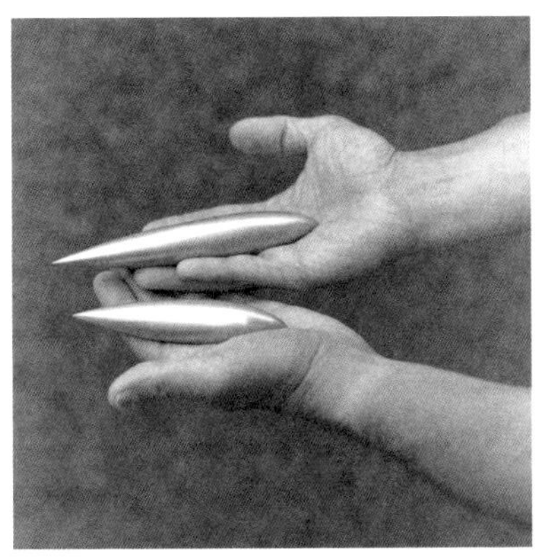
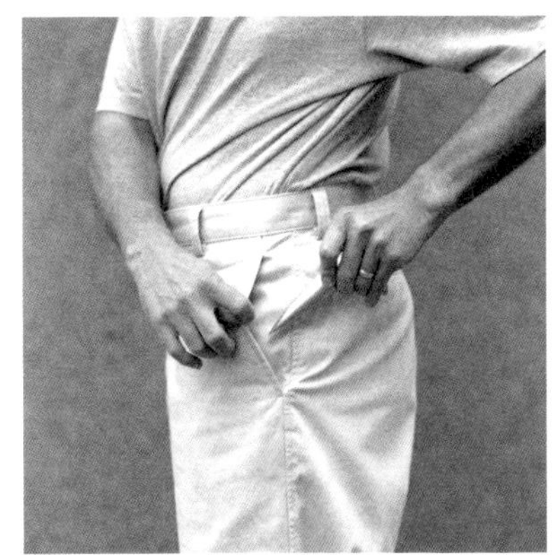
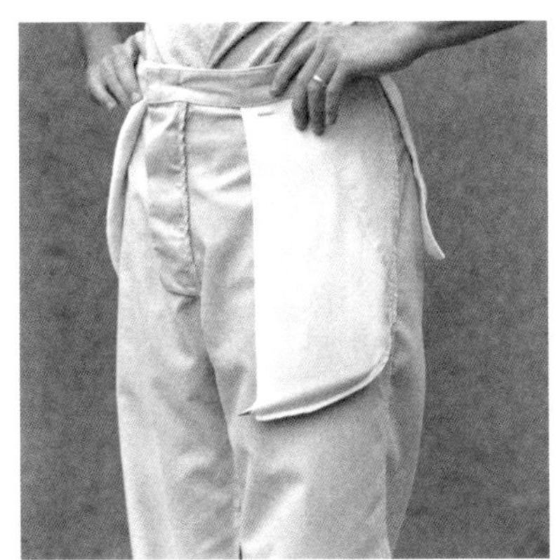
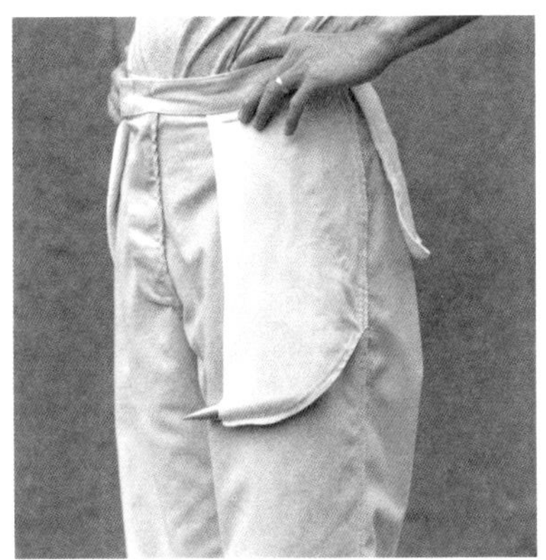
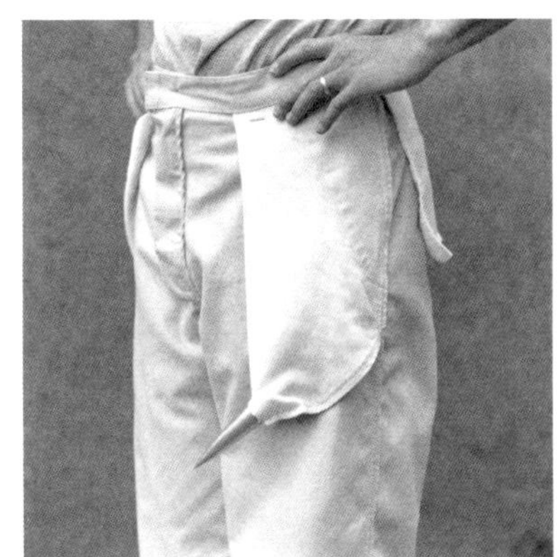

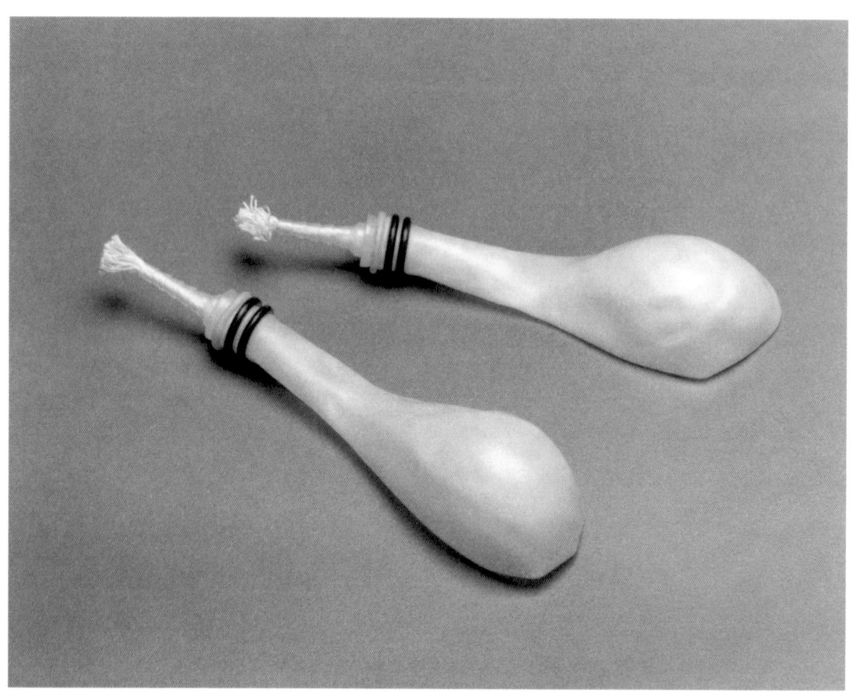

Pocket Water Bladders

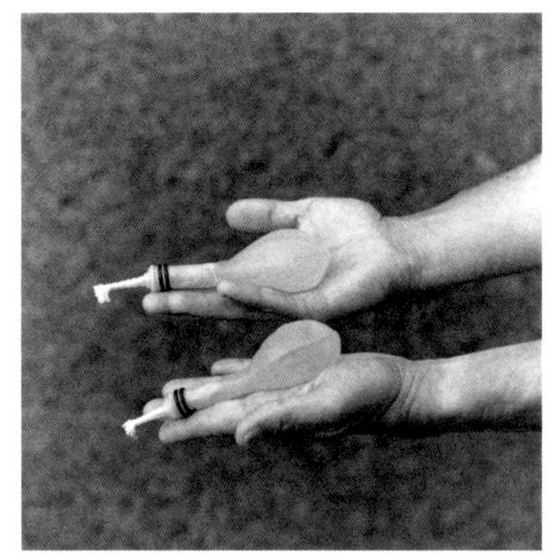

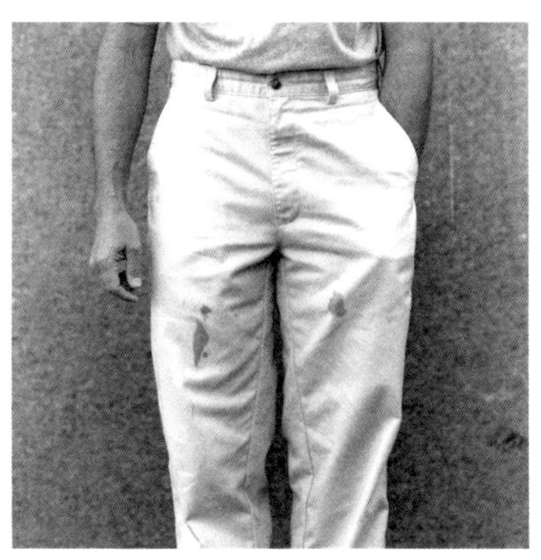
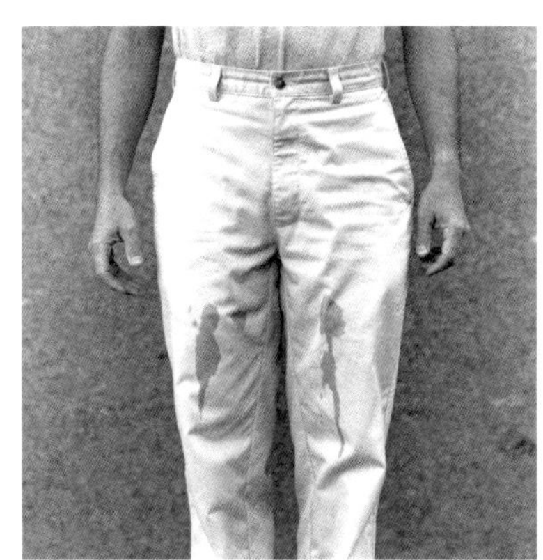
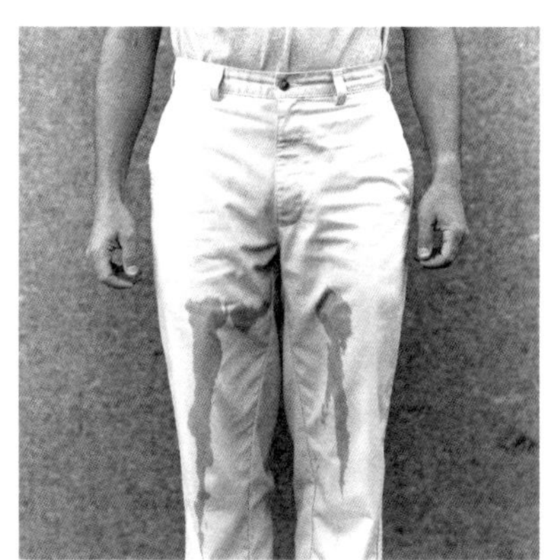

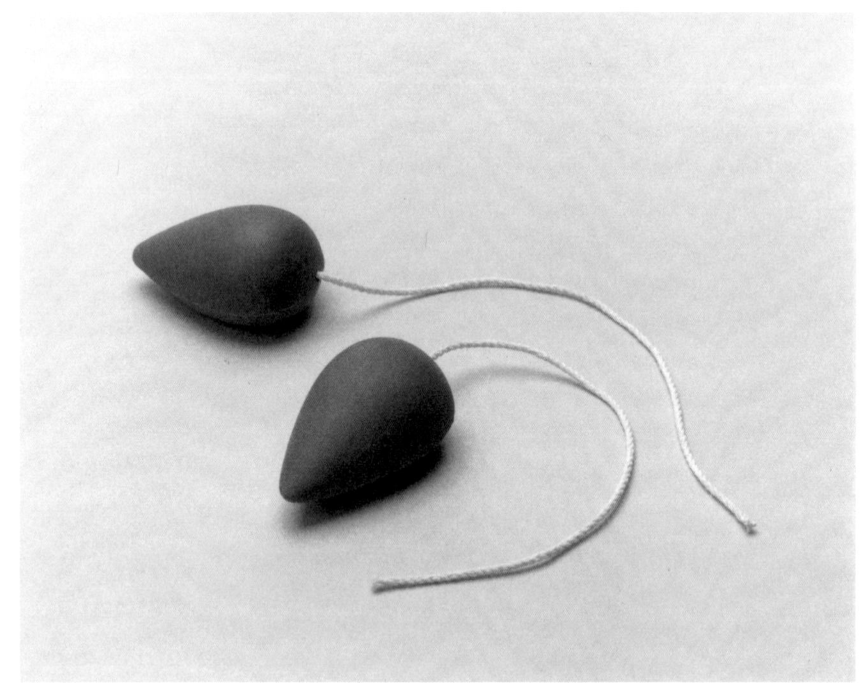

Chocolate Pocket Mice

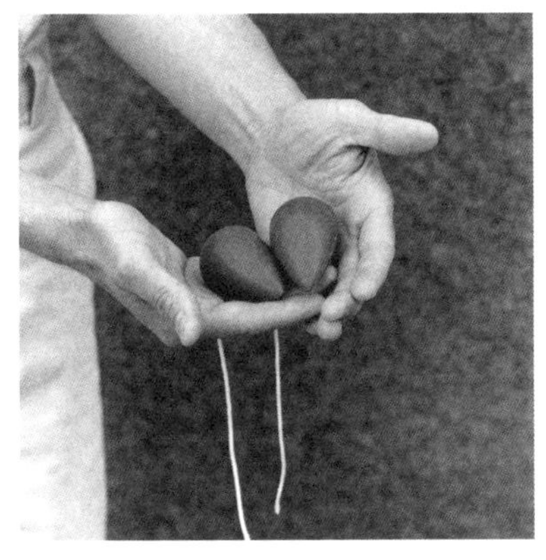
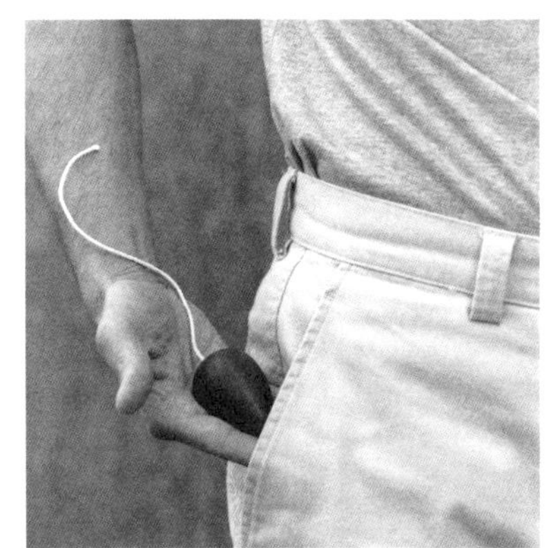
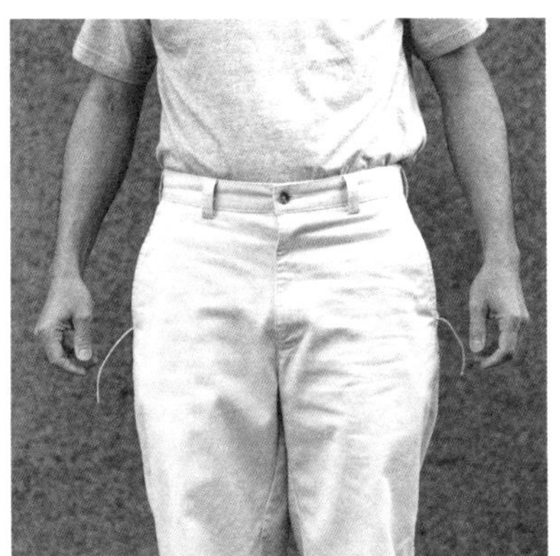
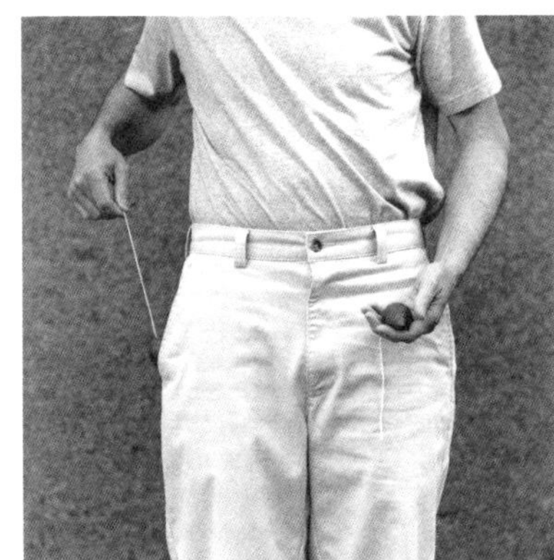
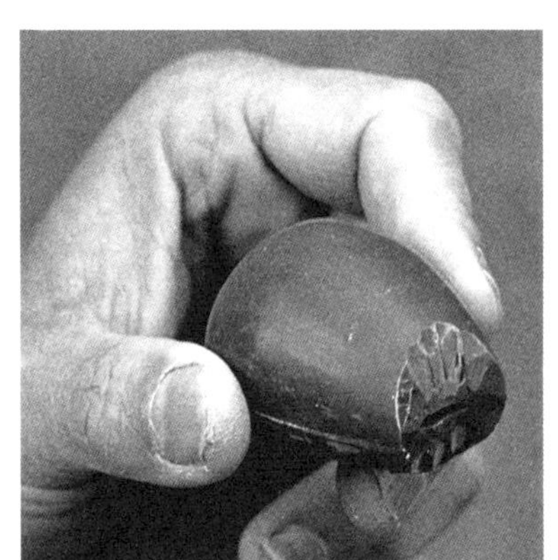

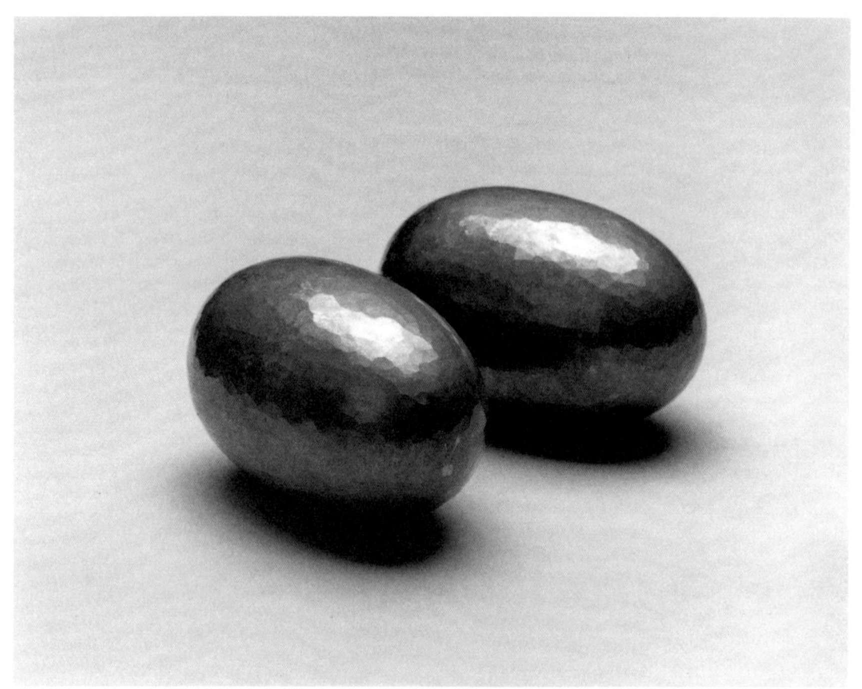

Lead Pocket Eggs

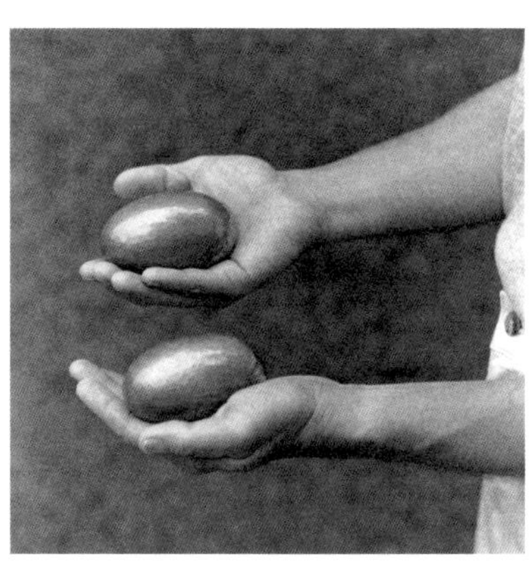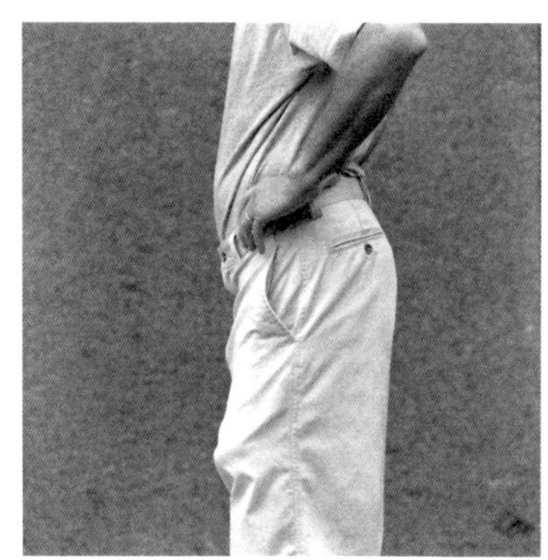

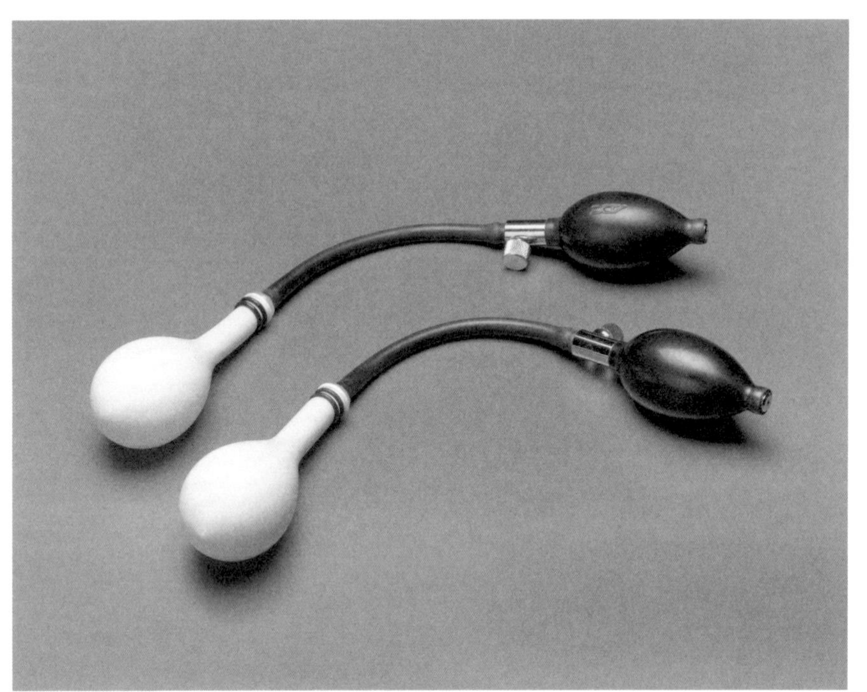

Pocket Air Bags

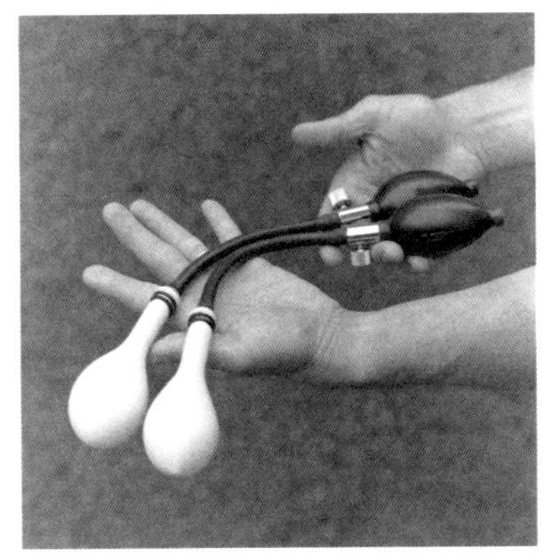

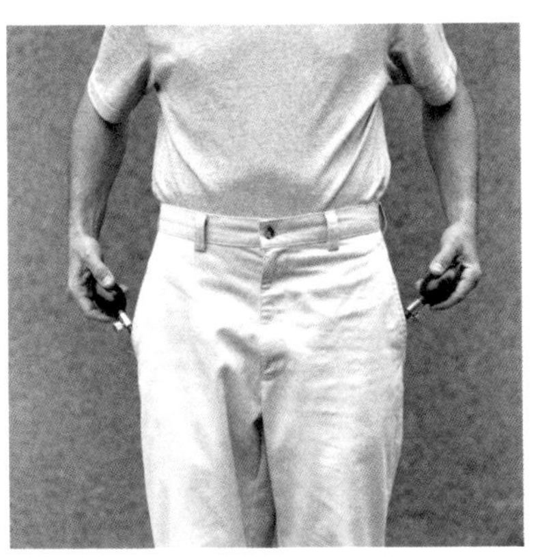

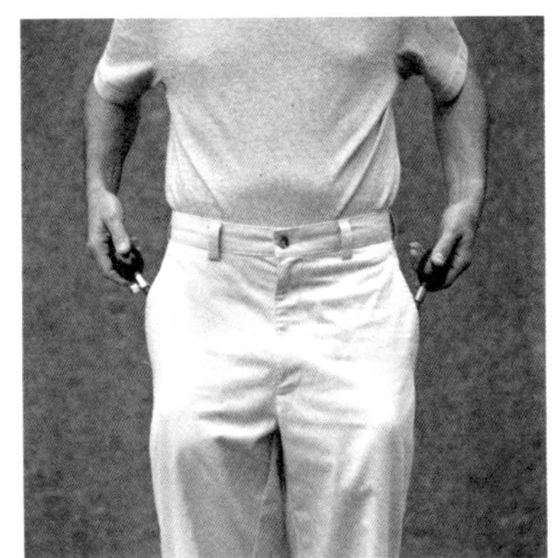

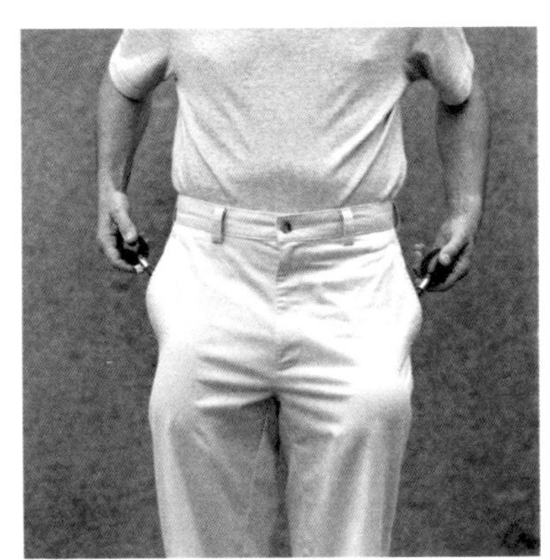

Works in the Exhibition

Jonathan Bonner
American, b. 1947
Philadelphia College of Art, BFA 1971;
Rhode Island School of Design,
MFA 1973

Object Pairs

*Measurements in inches; height precedes
width precedes length, unless otherwise
indicated. Order of entries matches order
of preceding photographs.*

Graphite Pocket Balls, 1999
Graphite
Left: 1⅞ (diam.); right: 2¼ (diam.)

Pocket Magnets, 1999
Ceramic
Each: ½ x 2¾ (diam.)

Glass Pocket Balls, 1999
Glass
Left: 2 (diam.); right: 2½ (diam.)

Ice Pocket Mounds, 1999
Anodized aluminium (mold),
ice (when filled)
Each: 2½ x 4⅜ (diam.)

Pocket Counterweights, 2001
Blued steel, nylon
Each: 2¼ x 2 (diam.)
Each: 1 lb., 2 oz.
Cord: 60

Pocket Burr Balls with Insertion Tube, 1999
Burrs from the common burdock plant
Each: 2 (diam., irregular)
PVC plastic (insertion tube)
2 (diam.) x 12½ (fully inserted)

Pocket Weasels, 1999
Stainless steel
Left: 1 (max. diam.) x 4¾;
right: 1 (max. diam.) x 6

Pocket Water Bladders, 1999
Latex, nylon, cotton
Each: 1⅛ x 1¾ (deflated balloon) x 6

Chocolate Pocket Mice, 2001
Chocolate, cotton
Each: 1⅜ x 1¼ x 11

Lead Pocket Eggs, 1999
Lead
Each: 2¼ (max. diam.) x 3⅝
Each: 3 lb., 9 oz.

Pocket Air Bags, 1999
Latex, nylon, stainless steel
Each: 1⅞ (max. diam. of squeezer)
x 14½

Video

Color video, silent
5:33 minutes
DVD player, LCD screen

Afterword

Jonathan Bonner and Richard Serra are unlikely bedfellows. I was, therefore, taken by surprise when Bonner told me that the initial impetus for *Front Pockets* was a comment by Serra about "audience." In a 1980 interview by Douglas Crimp, Serra talked about a sculpture he had made ten years earlier for a city street in New York: "The place in the Bronx was sinister, used by the local criminals to torch the cars they'd stolen. There was no audience for the sculpture in the Bronx, and it was my misconception that the so-called art audience would seek the work out" (Richard Serra, *Writings Interviews*. Chicago/London: 1994, p. 128). Bonner, a sculptor trained in woodworking, furniture design, and metalsmithing, was stimulated by Serra's remark to explore the nature of the smallest possible audience for an artwork.

In direct response to Serra – an artist known for large-scale, abstract, site-specific works in steel whose intent is to bring viewers into the sculpture – Bonner's *Front Pockets* focuses on the relationship between an individual and pairs of objects that fit into his or her trouser pockets. It is a private relationship made public by placing the objects in a museum and publishing images of them in a book. While Serra expresses disappointment that neighborhood people ignored his artwork and sophisticated art aficionados did not bother to visit the Bronx site, Bonner good-naturedly provokes viewers to connect with his inventions.

Front Pockets consists of eleven pairs of objects, a videotape, and this book. Both the video and the publication demonstrate the objects in use. Working with a videographer, a photojournalist, and a product photographer, Bonner has tried to achieve a presentation that is as neutral as possible, to make obvious the function of each type of object with minimal text and without sound, so that the viewer is free to provide additional content and to identify with the process. The object pairs – magnets, weights, balls – have some relationship to everyday use; but their functionality is preposterous. The sharply elongated "weasels" cut through the cloth of the pockets, the ice in the breast-shaped mounds melts and soaks the front of the pants, the air bags are inflated until they burst, and so on.

Bonner's objects are masterfully conceived, designed, and crafted, but the artist is much more interested in the long-standing relationship of hands to pockets and genitals than in

the idea of function. Personal items to
which we require easy access (keys,
money, Kleenex, pillboxes) are kept
in front pockets. Like underwear, they
are close to our bodies and out of
public view. By putting the exhibited
objects into his own pockets, manipu-
lating or playing with them until their
function is revealed to the point of
absurdity, and recording the sequence,
Bonner asks each viewer to identify
with this experience and become aware
of his or her responses. Wit, humor,
and mischief replace shame and embar-
rassment. The sculptor/performance
artist Janine Antoni made a hanging
sculpture, *Grope*, 1990–95, from 208
men's work-pants pockets. Her aim of
making visible what is normally hidden
resonates with Bonner's intent.

Front Pockets was conceived for a
museum setting. In order to connect
Bonner's contemporary inventions

with historic artifacts and museological
categories, each pair of objects is dis-
played on a separate pedestal covered
by a Plexiglas vitrine, elevated and
isolated to invite scrutiny, and lit to
accentuate its nature as sculpture,
artifact, and product. The deadpan
but hilarious video, which was shot in
the style of an industrial promotion,
is played on an LCD screen on the
twelfth pedestal, so that museum
visitors may observe how the objects
are deployed. Bonner utilizes the
conventions of display at the same time
that he subtly pokes fun at them in a
way similar to his humorous swipes at
functionalism.

The performer in the photographs and the video is a white male
seen from chest to knee, but he pres-
ents no other distinguishing features,
nor does the background against
which he appears. He wears unpleated

light-colored casual pants and a plain
t-shirt, another conscious choice by
Bonner to achieve neutrality. One
may surmise that the activator of the
objects is the artist, but by not identify-
ing himself, Bonner directs attention
to the viewer's own experience and
reactions. Combining the roles of
artist, industrial designer, and stand-
up comic, Bonner invites us to think
about the most basic everyday activi-
ties and to pay attention to the innu-
merable objects – both simple and
elaborate, useful and pointless – that
define our "civilization."

JUDITH TANNENBAUM
Curator of Contemporary Art
Museum of Art
Rhode Island School of Design

Library of Congress Control No. 2001135501
ISBN 0-911517-73-1

3,000 copies for the Museum of Art, Rhode Island School of Design, Providence
on the occasion of the exhibition *Jonathan Bonner: Front Pockets*
November 9, 2001 – January 27, 2002

Object photographs: Ric Murray
Demonstration photographs: Bill Gallery
Video: Geoff Adams
Text editing: Judith A. Singsen, Museum of Art, Rhode Island School of Design, Providence
Design and typography: Gilbert Design Associates, Inc., Providence
Printing: Meridian Printing, East Greenwich
Binding: Acme Bookbinding Co., Inc., Charlestown

This exhibition was made possible in part by a grant from The Concordia Foundation.